Atkins [

The Top 100 Atkins Recipes f

Amie Frances

Copyright © 2016

All legal rights reserved. You cannot offer this book for free or sell it. You do not have reselling legal rights to this book. This eBook may not be recreated in any file format or physical format without having the expressed written approval. All Violators will be sued.

While efforts have been made to assess that the information contained in this book is valid, neither the author nor the publisher assumes any accountability for errors, interpretations, omissions or usage of the subject matters herein.

Summary

High Protein Cheesecake 7
Blueberry Ice Cream 8
Flan 8
Fruity Protein Pudding 9
Chocolate Drizzled Meringue Cookies 9
Strawberry Vanilla Cake 10
Fresh Broccoli Soup 11
Free Bread 11
Chocolate Mocha Protein Shake 12
Home made Almond Milk 13
Mochachino 13
Protein Chai Latte 14
Dark Protein Shake 15
Protein Shake 15
Cajun Spice 16
Moroccan Spice 17
Salad Dressing Recipe 17
Fat-Free Mayo 18
Dill Garlic Dip 18
Superb BBQ Marinade 19
Fajita Fiesta Spice Mix 19
Italian Seasoning 20
Asian Dressing 20
Veggie Dressing 21
Protein Oatmeal Pudding 21

Chocolate-Berry Protein Oatmeal 22

Protein Cinnamon Oatmeal 22

Gluten Free Squash Pancakes 23

Zucchini Pancakes 24

Banana Oatmeal Pancakes..25

Chia Seed Cereal 25

Ground Turkey Omelet 26

Egg White Mushroom Omelet 27

Blueberry Oatmeal Pancakes 28

Southwestern Omelet...28

Baked Seafood Omelet 29

High Protein Pancake 30

Protein Waffles..31

Quinoa Burgers...32

Low Carb Tortillas...33

Chicken Shawarma Lettuce Wraps 33

High Protein Pizza 34

Turkey Meatballs..36

Pork Pico De Gallo 37

Stuffed Peppers..38

Baked Chicken Balls 39

Garlic Mashed Cauliflower..40

Chicken Spaghetti Squash 40

Lemon Curry Halibut 41

Tuna Burgers..42

Spicy Chicken Breast Chili 43

Baked Sweet French Fries 43

Frittata 44

Fettuccini Alfredo 45

Garlic Lime Chicken Fajitas 46

Fish Muffins 47

Stuffed Tomatoes with Cottage Cheese & Egg 48

Baked Broccoli Loaf 49

Mushroom Burgers with Shrimp 49

Spicy Mexican Stir Fry 50

African Style Vegetable Medley 51

Pasta Free Lasagna 52

Chicken Shawarma Lettuce Wraps 54

Tuna Cucumber Roll 55

Asian Salmon Steaks 55

Sushi 56

Chicken Tacos Salad 57

Tom Soup 58

Bun-Much less Mushroom Cheese Burgers 59

Chicken Meatloaf 60

Breadless Crab Truffles 61

Grilled Citrus Flavored Chicken Breast 62

Shrimp Stuffed Tomato 62

Grilled Balsamic Basa 63

Mustard & Dill Broiled Salmon 64

Grilled Tomato Shrimp 64

Grilled Chicken Breast with Veggie Salsa 65

Turkey Breast Quick Wraps 66

Mexican Rissoles 67

Cucumber Radish Dill Salad 68

Fresh Quinoa Salad 69

Fresh Chicken Salad 69

Apple Cinnamon Protein Muffins 70

Protein Bars 70

Dairy Free Protein Bars 71

Protein Cupcakes 72

Gluten, Carb & Dairy Free Bread 73

Selfmade Protein Bars 74

Protein Cinnamon Cake with Cocoa Syrup 75

Frozen Yogurt 76

Blueberry Cookies 76

Cinnamon Oatmeal High Protein Frozen Pudding 77

Veggie & Egg Muffins 77

Zucchini Chips with Cajun Dip 78

Protein Fudge Balls 80

Hungarian Stew 80

Moroccan Style Chicken 81

Beef & Broccoli Stir Fry 82

Easy Chicken & Spinach Stir Fry 83

Stuffed Chicken Breast 84

Russian Stir-Fry 85

Low Carb Tacos 85

Chicken Breast Mushroom Sandwich 86

Cheese Wraps 87

High Protein Cheesecake

Ingredients

¾ C nonfat cottage cheese
2/three C nonfat plain yogurt
1 tbsp. oat flour
5 packets stevia
¼ tsp. salt
four egg whites
Juice from ½ a lemon
½ C blueberries
1oz chopped pecans (optional)

Directions
1. Preheat oven to 350° F.
2. Mix cottage cheese, yogurt, oat flour, stevia, salt & lemon juice in a blender till smooth & creamy.
3. Add egg whites to the combination & pulse a few times.
4. Remove blender from the bottom & add the berries & stir in the combination with a spoon (don't mix the berries).
5. Spray the bottom of your pan (or use muffin tin) with some cooking spray & line with chopped pecans for crust.
6. Pour the batter combination in.
7. Bake for roughly half-hour checking frequently to ensure the cheesecake doesn't brown or dry out.
8. Chill the cake in the fridge for a few hours.

Blueberry Ice Cream

Ingredients

1 C fat free cottage cheese
1/three C frozen blueberries
Stevia (to taste)
1 tsp. natural vanilla extract
¼ C of unsweetened almond milk

Directions
1. Mix all of the ingredients to form a paste.
2. Put it in a bowl & enjoy

YouCeven make a smoothie out of the same ingredients. Merely, add 1 extra C of unsweetened almond milk.

Flan

Ingredients

½ envelope gelatin
1 C unsweetened almond milk
1 scoop of whey protein isolate powder
stevia (optional)

Directions
1. In a big bowl mix protein powder & gelatin.
2. Add warm almond milk.
3. Whisk.
4. Pour the combination in 2 dishes of equal size & refrigerate overnight.

Fruity Protein Pudding

Ingredients

1 packet sugar free Jell-O (decide any flavor)
1 C zero fat free cottage cheese
2 tbsp. ground flax seeds

Directions
1. Mix the ingredients together.
2. Refrigerate for half-hour & enjoy.

Chocolate Drizzled Meringue Cookies

Ingredients

1 c egg whites
2 tsp. organic vanilla extract
1 tbsp. cinnamon
Stevia (to taste)
1 C melted cottage cheese
1 tbsp. `cocoa powder

Directions
1. Preheat the oven to 350 degrees Celsius.
2. Beat the egg whites with a mixer, till they foam.
3. Add vanilla, stevia & cinnamon & beat the egg whites some more, till the foam will get firmer.

4. With a spoon, scoop out the batter & place it on a baking sheet sprayed with Pam (you must have roughly 36 spoonful's).
5. Put in the oven & bake for 20 minutes.
6. Meanwhile, mix cottage cheese, cocoa powder & stevia together.
7. Once the cookies are prepared, take them out of the oven & let cool for 10 minutes.
8. Top each cookie with the cottage cheese combination & enjoy.

Strawberry Vanilla Cake

Ingredients

four scoops of Vanilla whey protein isolate
Stevia (to taste)
2 tsp. baking powder
1 tbsp. organic vanilla extract
1 pack sugar free Strawberry Jell-O
1 C fat free low sodium cottage cheese, strained & mashed (get a cheese cloth & drain the cottage cheese chunks from the liquid, then mash the chunks)

Directions

1. In a microwave pleasant bowl, mix protein powder, cottage cheese, stevia, baking powder & vanilla extract.
2. Add ¾ c water & mix well.
3. Microwave the batter for ninety seconds.
4. Take out the batter & crush it.

5. Mix Jell-O with ¾ c of hot water & pour it into the crushed batter.
6. Cover the dish with saran wrap & chill through the night time.
7. Cut into eight slices & serve.

Fresh Broccoli Soup

Ingredients

1 leek
1 bunch of coriander
four green onions
2 floretscups of broccoli
½ of a medium cauliflower
2 cloves of garlic
eight cups of spinach leaves
¼ C lemon juice
1 tsp. ground Ginger
Sea salt & cracked pepper to taste
½ C water

Directions
1. Heat all ingredients (besides coriander & spinach) in a deep saucepan or a wok.
2. Permit to simmer for 20-half-hour, add coriander & spinach last.
3. Use a hand-held blender to mix it to desired thickness.

Free Bread

Ingredients

1. 300g almond meal
    four tbsp. olive oil
    1 tsp. baking powder
    6 egg whites
    stevia to taste
    2 tsp. of cinnamon

Directions
1. Mix all of the ingredients together to make a dough.
2. Form right into a loaf form into your baking tin.
3. Bake for round 30min on 200 degrees Celsius.
4. Let cool the loaf cool for 20 minutes & take away from tin.
5. Enjoy!

Chocolate Mocha Protein Shake

Ingredients

1 tsp. prompt coffee (Nestle Vanilla or Hazelnut flavor is the very best!)
1½ scoops chocolate whey protein powder
1 C non sweetened Almond Milk (Vanilla or Chocolate)
½ C non fat yogurt
½ tsp. cocoa powder
2 packets stevia
1-2 cups ice cubes

Directions
Mix all ingredients right into a blender & mix for about 30 seconds on high.

Home made Almond Milk

Ingredients

2 cups raw almonds
three liters Spring water
Stevia (to taste)

Directions
1. Soak the almonds in spring water overnight.
2. Put 1 C of almonds & three cups of water (the one during which the almonds have been soaked) in a blender.
3. Add stevia.
4. Mix the ingredients.
5. Strain the liquid through a cheesecloth or a straining bag right into a bottle or a pitcher.
6. Repeat with the remaining of the almonds.

Almond milk has been a staple in our weight-reduction plan for a very long time. We add it to coffee & tea, as well as into recipes. You may also enjoy this scrumptious beverage by itself, so long as your macro nutrient intake permits you.

Mochachino

Ingredients

Nestea Vanilla or Hazelnut Flavored Instantaneous coffee
Liquid Stevia (the most effective is the English Toffee Flavored one by Sweet Leaf)
½ C of non-sweetened vanilla Almond Milk
1 tsp. unsweetened cocoa powder

Directions
1. Make prompt coffee but only use half the quantity of water.
2. Microwave (or heat on stovetop) almond milk for about 1 min till warm but not boiling hot.
3. Place almond milk, coco & about eight drops of liquid stevia in a blender or Magic Bullet.
4. Mix till the combination appears foamy.
5. Add the foamy almond milk combination to your coffee & stir
   So good!

Protein Chai Latte

Ingredients

1 Chai Tea bag
1 scoop Whey Protein Isolate Powder (Vanilla is an effective choice right here)
1 C of non-sweetened vanilla Almond Milk (optional)
Stevia to taste if desired

Directions
1. Boil water or almond milk
2. Add tea bag, let stand for a couple of minutes (depending how strong you want your tea), remove tea bag.
3. Add protein & stevia & mix for a couple of minutes.
   YouCeven enjoy this cold, just await tea to chill before adding protein or cool & add ice for an ice chai tea

latte *Nutrient breakdown per serving with almond milk (varies primarily based in your protein shake - check label):*

Dark Protein Shake

Ingredients

½ C cottage cheese
½ scoop of whey protein isolate powder (any flavor goes!)
Stevia to taste (optional)
three ice cubes
Water (put much less in case you need the shake to be thicker)
½ tsp xanthan gum

Choices:
If you're still consuming fat add ½ avocado or a tbsp. of any of the next: natural peanut butter/almond butter/hazelnut butter/flax seed oil.

Additional choices:
1 tbsp. of cocoa powder, 1tsp cinnamon, 1 C spinach (in case you are not utilizing cocoa powder, they do not work together).

Directions
1. Mix all ingredients together & enjoy.

Protein Shake

Ingredients

2 tbsp. hazelnut instantaneous coffee

goes) 1 scoop whey isolate powder (any flavor but fruit

1 C almond milk

Directions
1. Merely mix all of the ingredients & enjoy!
2. If you're utilizing ephedrine & caffeine as a fat burner, just throw the ephedrine tabs in the combination & mix. Make certain to thoroughly shake it for the tabs to dissolve.
3. If you're nearing the present & wish to chop the additional carbs out, replace the almond milk for water.
4. You tooCadd the whey & ½ C almond milk right into a hot coffee. If you purchase your coffee from a coffee store, ensure that the quantity of caffeine doesn't exceed 200mg.

Cajun Spice

Ingredients

¼ C paprika
¼ C salt
three tbsp.s black pepper
three tbsp.s garlic powder
1 tbsp. onion powder
2 tsp.s cayenne
1 ½ tsp.s dried oregano
1 ½ tsp.s dried thyme

Directions

1. Mix all ingredients.
2. Store in an air tight container & keep in a cool, dark place.

Moroccan Spice

Ingredients

¼ C tsp. garlic powder
¼ C tsp. chili
three tbsp. cumin
1 tsp. cinnamon

Directions
1. Mix all ingredients.
2. Store in an air tight container & keep in a cool, dark place.

Salad Dressing Recipe

Ingredients

1 C flax oil
1 C apple cider vinegar
1 tbsp. dried mustard
1 tbsp. fresh garlic
Minced dill to taste

Directions

Merely mix all of the ingredients together & store in the fridge for at the very least a day before use.

Fat-Free Mayo

Ingredients

6 oz. zero% Plain Greek Yogurt
¼ tsp. Cider Vinegar
1/eight tsp. Yellow Mustard
1 dash Hot Pepper Sauce
1 dash White Pepper
1 dash Paprika
1 dash Salt

Directions

Mix all ingredients together & mix well. Adjust to swimsuit taste.

Dill Garlic Dip

Ingredients

½ Greek yogurt
2 garlic cloves, mashed
¼ C dill
1 tsp. onion powder

Directions

Merely mix all of the ingredients in a bowl & serve with your dipping food of choice, i.e. cucumbers, celery, sweet potato French Fries.

You may as well use it as a ramification in your Ezekiel bread or on the lettuce leaves for wraps. The chances are countless!

Superb BBQ Marinade

Ingredients

¼ red onion, sliced
three garlic cloves minced
1 tsp. salt
1 tsp. ground white pepper
1 tsp. freshly ground black pepper
1 tsp. paprika
1 tsp. dried basil
1 tsp. Worcestershire sauce
¼ C lemon juice
½ cups red wine vinegar
½ cups olive oil

Directions
1. Mix all ingredients till well blended.
2. Pour over food, & marinate overnight.

Fajita Fiesta Spice Mix

Ingredients

2 tsp. chili powder
1 tsp. salt
1 tsp. paprika
¼ tsp. powdered stevia
¾ tsp. crushed chicken bouillon cube
½ tsp. onion powder
¼ tsp. garlic powder
¼ tsp. cayenne pepper
¼ tsp. cumin

Directions

1. Mix all ingredients in a small bowl.
2. Use as needed in recipes calling for fajita seasoning.

Italian Seasoning

Ingredients

three tsp. dried basil
three tsp. dried oregano
three tbsp. dried parsley
1 tsp. garlic powder
1 tsp. onion powder
1 tsp. dried thyme
1 tsp. dried rosemary
¼ tsp. black pepper
¼ tsp. red pepper flakes

Directions
1. Mix all ingredients in a spice grinder or put in a small bowl & crush with the back of a spoon.

Asian Dressing

Ingredients

2 garlic cloves
1 tbsp. of minced fresh ginger
2 green onions, minced
¼ C chicken broth/stock
2 tbsp. rice wine vinegar
1 tbsp. soy sauce (really useful: organic fermented & low sodium)
1 tbsp. sesame oil

Directions
1. Mix all ingredients in a blender, or process in a food processor, or mince garlic & easily mix everything along with a fork.

Veggie Dressing

Ingredients

½ C coconut oil
¾ C apple cider vinegar
2 packets powder stevia
1 tbsp. basil
½ tsp. ground black pepper
2-three cloves of garlic
Salt to taste

Directions
1. Mix all ingredients in a blender, or process in a food processor, or mince garlic & easily mix everything along with a fork.

Protein Oatmeal Pudding

Ingredients

½ C of Oats
1 scoop of Whey Isolate Protein Powder
½ C of Unsweetened Almond Milk (optional)

Directions
1. Mix oats with the almond milk.
2. Microwave on high setting for 1-2 minutes, till the oatmeal is of a little runny consistency.
3. Add the protein powder.

Chocolate-Berry Protein Oatmeal

Ingredients

½ C Dry Oats
four egg whites
½ scoop of Whey Protein Isolate Powder
1 tsp. of Pure Cocoa Powder
2 packets of Stevia
1 tbsp. of Flax Oil
½ C of Frozen Combined Berries
¼ C of Water

Directions
1. In a giant bowl, mix all of the ingredients (apart from the frozen Berries).
2. Microwave on high setting for 1-2 minutes, till the oatmeal is of a little runny consistency.
3. Once cooked, add the frozen berries, stir & enjoy.

Makes 1 serving. Nutrient breakdown per serving:
17

Protein Cinnamon Oatmeal

Ingredients

½ C of oats
6 egg whites
¼ tsp. of cinnamon
5-6 drops of liquid vanilla stevia or 1-2 packets of dry stevia

Directions
1. Mix all ingredients with the oats.
2. Microwave on high setting for 1-2 minutes, till the oatmeal is of a little runny consistency.
   Makes 1 serving.
   Nutrient breakdown per serving:
   18

Gluten Free Squash Pancakes

Ingredients

2 cups Cooked Squash or Pumpkin
1 C Chopped Spinach
1 C Minced Onion
¼ C Almond Flour
½ tsp. Sea Salt
12 egg whites
1 tsp. Coconut Oil

Directions
1. In case you're utilizing cooked spaghetti squash, place it in a bowl & separate the strands with a fork. In case you're utilizing one other number of cooked squash or pumpkin, puree it in a food processor or

blender (keep the squash a bit chunky) & transfer to a bowl.
2. Mix in the onion, flour, & salt. Lightly beat the eggs & add them to the squash combination.
3. Heat a skillet or griddle over medium heat. Lightly grease the pan with oil. Use a ¼ C measure to scoop the batter into the hot pan.
4. Cook the pancakes till they develop a very crunchy crust - they'll keep delightfully chewy on the inside.

Zucchini Pancakes

Ingredients

1 tbsp. Coconut Flour
three whole eggs
Sea Salt & Pepper
(plus another fresh spices & herbs to your taste)
2 cups Shredded Zucchini
1 tsp. Coconut Oil

Directions
1. Sift the coconut flour into the eggs & beat them together
2. Mix in the shredded zucchini, sea salt & pepper
3. Use a big forged iron or chrome steel skillet over medium-low heat with coconut oil coating the pan
4. Spoon the combination into the pan in size of pancake you need
5. Cook for a couple of minutes & flip over when golden brown

Banana Oatmeal Pancakes

Ingredients

1.5 cups Unsweetened Almond Milk
1 C Rolled Oats
1 Banana
½ C of Almond Flour
1 tsp. of Baking Powder

1 tbsp. Non Fat Plain Greek Yogurt
5-eight drops of Liquid Stevia
2 tbsp. Blueberries

Directions
1. In a blender, puree 1 ½ C of almond milk & 1 C of rolled oats till smooth
2. Add banana, almond flour & 1 tea spoon of baking powder
3. Let sit for 10 min
4. Meanwhile mix topping ingredients together
5. Make a pancake on a non stick pan

Chia Seed Cereal

Ingredients

1 C of Organic Rolled Oats
1 tsp. of Cinnamon

1 tbsp. of Chia Seeds
Few drops of Stevia
1 C of Almond Milk
1 scoop of Whey Protein Isolate

Directions
1. Boil/microwave the oatmeal with almond milk
2. Add all of the remaining ingredients

Makes 1 serving. Nutrient breakdown per serving:
22

Ground Turkey Omelet

Ingredients

eight egg whites
2 large whole eggs
2 Small, Raw Onions, Diced
three oz. Ground, Raw Turkey
1 C Chopped Green Bell Peppers
1 C Chopped Red Bell Peppers
1 C Raw Mushrooms, Sliced
three tbsp. Extra Virgin Olive Oil
1 dash Ground Black Pepper
1 tsp. Hot Pepper Sauce
three cloves Raw Garlic, Minced
1 tsp. Ground Turmeric
1 tsp. Worcestershire Sauce

Directions
1. Sauté turkey, greens & spices, besides turmeric, with 1tsp of olive oil till tender.

2. Whip the eggs, egg whites & turmeric together.
3. Pre-heat 2 tsp. of olive oil in a second skillet, then add ½ egg combination & cook to form an omelet. Repeat to make 2 omelets.
4. Place 1 omelet on plate, top with ½ of the turkey combination, & roll it to form a wrap. 5. Repeat the same process with the opposite omelet.

Egg White Mushroom Omelet

Ingredients

12 egg whites
1 C Grated Zucchini
1 tbsp. Paprika
1 tsp. Fresh Oregano
1 C Sliced Mushrooms
1 C of Spinach
Salt, Pepper (to taste)

Directions
1. Mix all of the ingredients, except for mushrooms, in a blender.
2. Pour it on a hot pan lightly greased with coconut oil.
3. Cook it like an omelet.
4. When almost prepared, add the mushrooms on top.
5. Cook till the mushrooms are prepared.
6. Serve & Enjoy!

Blueberry Oatmeal Pancakes

Ingredients

½ C Frozen Blueberries
1 C Oats
1 tsp. Baking Powder
1 C Almond Milk (Unsweetened)
12 egg whites
1 C Unsweetened Applesauce
Stevia (to taste)
2 tsp. of Cinnamon

Directions

1. Mix stevia, egg whites, baking powder, almond milk, salt & oats.
2. Add ¼ of the blueberries to the combination.
3. Cook the pancakes on a lightly oiled pan over medium heat.
4. Top with a mix of applesauce, cinnamon & stevia.

Southwestern Omelet

Ingredients

1/three C Mushrooms Chopped
1/three C Green Onion
1-2 Garlic Cloves Minced
6 egg whites
½ tsp. Chili Powder
Salt & Pepper to Taste
1/three C Spinach Chopped

¼ C Fat-Free Cottage Cheese

2 tbsp. Salsa (search for ones whichCbe low carb with no sugar or oils added)

1 tsp. Coconut Oil

Directions
1. Lightly oil a pan & let it heat over high setting.
2. Add mushrooms, green onion, garlic & sauté till soft. Put aside on a plate.
3. Mix egg whites with chili powder, salt & pepper.
4. Oil the pan once more & pour the egg whites in. Instantly add the cooked veggies on top of the egg whites
5. Cover the pan & let cook. Once the top of the eggs is considerably solid you should utilize a spatula to flip the omelet over.
6. Cook an extra minute & take away from heat.
7. Top the omelet with chopped spinach, cottage cheese & salsa, & fold.

Baked Seafood Omelet

Ingredients

100g Cooked Shrimp
four egg whites
2 tbsp. Melted Fat Free Cottage Cheese
½ tsp. Tarragon
Salt & Pepper to taste
1 tsp. Coconut Oil

Directions
1. Preheat oven to 375.

2. In a bowl, whisk eggs, tarragon & cottage cheese together.
3. Pour the contents of the bowl onto a skillet oiled with coconut oil.
4. Once the omelet creates a base add the shrimp on top.
5. Place the skillet on the top shelf of the oven & bake for five minutes.
6. Take the omelet out of the oven, fold in half & enjoy!

High Protein Pancake

Ingredients

½ scoop of Whey Protein Isolate Powder
¼ tsp. Baking Powder
2 tbsp. Ground Flaxseed
four egg whites
1 tsp. Coconut Oil

Directions

1. Lightly oil a medium sized nonstick pan with coconut oil.
2. Mix or mix (greater if blended) all above ingredients together.
3. Once the pan is hot, pour half the batter into the pan & cover.
4. Let cook for three-four minutes checking often so it doesn't burn.
5. Once the top of the pancake appears to be like solid flip it over & cook the opposite side for an additional 30-60 seconds.
   Topping Choices:

1. ¼ tsp. Cinnamon combined with 2-three packets of Stevia
2. 1 tsp. unsweetened cocoa powder combined with 2-three tbsp. nonfat plain yogurt, 10-15 drops of liquid stevia (adjust to taste), a few drops of vanilla extract
3. Peanut, Macadamia, walnut or almond butters

Protein Waffles

Ingredients

2 scoops of Whey Protein Isolate (any flavor)
four egg whites
½ C Oats, blended into flour
2 packets of Stevia
1 tsp. Cinnamon
1 tsp. Coconut Oil

Directions
1. Beat the egg whites
2. Add cinnamon, oat flour, stevia & cinnamon & mix well
3. Cook on a preheated waffle maker sprayed with Pam for three minutes
4. In the meantime, mix all of the topping ingredients
5. Once the waffles are prepared, pour the topping over them & enjoy!

Topping Choices:
1. 2 tbsp. Almond Milk
2. 2 packets Of Stevia
3. 1 tsp. Cinnamon

Quinoa Burgers

What you need

1 Large Onion
1 Clove Garlic
four cups Broccoli Bunch
1 medium Zucchini
1 C Green Beans
1 ½ C of Quinoa
three Cups Water
1 C Sliced Mushrooms
1 tsp. Coconut Oil
1 Lemon
1 C Quinoa Flakes
2 Whole Eggs – Beaten
Spice Choices – Cumin, pepper, turmeric, saffron, chili flakes
Fresh Herb Choices – Basil, coriander, parsley
1 C almond flour

Directions
1. Place water & quinoa in a saucepan till the water boils, reduce heat, cover & simmer for five minutes, drain quinoa if necessary.
2. In a non-stick pan, add coconut oil, onion, garlic, chosen spices & stir. Add all remaining greens. Once the greens have softened, add the quinoa, stir together. Add finely chopped chosen fresh herbs & lemon juice.
3. Have 2 separate bowls prepared – 1 with the beaten eggs, 1 with the almond flour & Quinoa flakes. Press the prepared made quinoa into spherical patties & cover in egg combination. Then roll the

patties into the almond flour/Quinoa mix, as in case you had been making burgers.
4. You will have to have a hot, non-stick frying pan or a grill prepared to cook the patties. Use 1 tsp. of coconut oil if needed.

Low Carb Tortillas

Ingredients

four.5 tbsp. Cottage Cheese
three medium eggs
1 tsp. Cream of Tartar
Pinch of Salt
1 tsp. Coconut Oil

Directions
1. Mix all ingredients together till the cottage cheese is pureed & you've got a smooth liquid.
2. Lightly oil a frying pan with coconut oil & heat over medium high heat.
3. Pour barely enough batter in the hot skillet to coat the bottom of the pan. Once the crepe strikes while you shake the pan (about 20 seconds), flip over & cook for an additional 10 seconds or till the crepe strikes while you shake the pan.
4. Repeat.

Chicken Shawarma Lettuce Wraps

What you need

1 C shredded English Cucumber
¼ C Non-Fat Plain Yogurt
1 tbsp. Tahini
2 tbsp. Lemon Juice
½ tsp. Salt, divided
1 tbsp. Garlic Powder
1 tsp. Curry Powder
½ tsp. Freshly Ground Pepper
1 lb. Boneless, Skinless Chicken Breast, trimmed
1 tbsp. Coconut Oil
Large Romaine Lettuce Leaves

Directions
1. Preheat grill to medium.
2. Stir cucumber, yogurt, tahini, lemon juice & ¼-tsp. salt together in a medium bowl. Put aside.
3. Mix garlic powder, curry powder, pepper & the remaining ¼-tsp. salt in one other medium bowl. Slice chicken breast crosswise into ¼-inch strips; toss with the spice combination to coat. Add 1-tbsp. oil & toss to mix.
4. Grill the chicken, turning once, till cooked through, about 2 minutes per side.
5. To serve, spread ¼ C of the cucumber-yogurt sauce on a big lettuce leaf & top with one-fourth of the chicken. Fold like a taco & enjoy!

High Protein Pizza

Ingredients

three medium zucchini, grated - per cup
1 egg, & four egg whites
1 C White Beans or Black Eyed Peas (mashed/blended to make a smooth consistency) if you wish to make this even
lower in carbs use 1 C cooked & mashed cauliflower
Salt & pepper to your choice

½ C Tomato Sauce (search for low carb/low sugar)
1 tsp. dry oregano
1 tsp. garlic powder
½ onion
2 C spinach
1 C mushrooms
½ red pepper
6 oz. chicken cooked breast
45g goat cheese (optional)

Directions
1. Preheat oven to 375F.
2. Spray a pizza pan with cooking spray (I just use a few pie trays & make individual pizzas).
3. Mix well grated zucchini, beans (or cauliflower) with egg & egg whites (or mix together), salt & pepper
4. Place zucchini/bean combination on the pizza pan spreading out to the edges of the pan.
5. Bake at 375F for half-hour.
6. Make pizza sauce by combining tomato sauce with oregano & garlic powder (add anything you want). Spread pizza sauce on partially-cooked "crust" to inside about ½ inch of the edge.

7. Dice veggies & chicken & mix with goat cheese. Add toppings to the pizza.
8. Bake for an additional half-hour or till cheese is melted & veggies are tender & cooked to your liking.
9. YouCactually experiment with this recipe by adding a variation of toppings & spices. Get inspirations from conventional pizza toppings & take a look at - BBQ pizza, meat lovers & many others.
10. If you employ pie trays, youCmerely cover with foil & store in the fridge which makes it very handy to seize one & go.

Turkey Meatballs

Ingredients

1 lemon - 1 tbsp. of grated lemon peel
2 green onions
2 garlic cloves
1 egg
2 tbsp. of chili garlic sauce or hot sauce
2 tsp. of fish sauce
1 lb. of ground turkey
three tsp. of cornstarch
2 tsp. of cilantro

Directions
1. Mix lemon grate, onion, garlic
2. Whisk egg, chili sauce & fish sauce & add to lemon/onion/garlic mix
3. Add turkey mix in
4. Add cornstarch & cilantro
5. Make meatballs & cook for 20-30min - four hundred diploma

Makes four servings. Nutrient breakdown per serving:

Pork Pico De Gallo

Ingredients

four extra lean pork chops (4oz each)
6 tbsp. of paprika - tsp. only
2 tbsp. ground pepper
2 tbsp. coarse salt
1 tbsp. chili powder
three pinches of cayenne

Directions

1. Mix paprika, pepper, salt, chili powder & cayenne together.
2. Rub combination into the pork.
3. Sear the pork chops then bake for about 15 min (350 degrees)

What you need

2 cups of black beans
three mediums tomatoes diced
½ C of red onion diced
½ C of green onion chopped
½ C of cilantro
2 tbsp. of jalapeno minced
2 tbsp. of lemon juice
1 tbsp. of chili powder

Directions

Mix all ingredients together. Serve pork chops/pork loin on mattress of arugula with pico de gallo.

Stuffed Peppers

Ingredients

6 large red or yellow bell peppers
2 medium onions
1.5 pounds of ground turkey
1C of diced tomatoes
1C of tomato paste
Black pepper
Himalayan salt
Paprika
Oregano
Dry parsley
250ml Fat Free Sour Cream

Directions

1. Preheat the oven to 350 degrees.
2. Cut the bell peppers in half vertically & discard all of the contents.
3. Cut onions into tiny pieces.
4. Mix the onions, diced tomatoes, black pepper, Himalayan salt, paprika, oregano & the parsley in a pan with the ground turkey & brown the meat.
5. Stuff the peppers with turkey mix (be certain to place loads).

6. Put the peppers in the oven & bake them for an hour.
7. Take the peppers out & serve with some sour cream on top.

Makes 6 servings. Nutrient breakdown per serving (per pepper).

Baked Chicken Balls

Ingredients

5-6 medium tomatoes
1 large onion
4lb of ground chicken
¼ C fresh cilantro
black pepper to taste
salt to taste

Directions

1. Preheat the oven for four hundred Celsius.
2. Dice the tomatoes (you should purchase canned ones, but I might steer clear of them, because of the preservatives).
3. Mince the onion.
4. Throw the onions & the tomatoes in a baking dish.
5. Chop up the cilantro.
6. Put the ground chicken right into a bowl.
7. Throw in & mix the cilantro, black pepper & salt.
8. Make chicken balls concerning the size of your fist.
9. Put them in the baking dish & cook it for an hour

Healthy, tasty & straightforward to make. Goes well with just about any side of your favorite carbs. Makes roughly 14 chicken balls.

Garlic Mashed Cauliflower

Ingredients

500g of fresh cauliflower - 1 medium head
2 cloves of fresh garlic
1cup fresh parsley
Salt & pepper (to taste)

What you do
1. Steam the cauliflower till it's soft. It must be easy to pierce it with a fork.
2. Crush the garlic utilizing garlic press.
3. Mash the cauliflower.
4. Mix in the garlic, parsley & spices.
5. Enjoy!

Chicken Spaghetti Squash

Ingredients

1 tsp Coconut Oil
1 C chopped onion
5 cloves minced garlic
1 C sliced mushrooms
1 C finely chopped fresh tomatoes

1 tbsp. dried basil
½ C fresh parsley
1 tbsp. dried oregano
1lb extra lean ground chicken
Salt & pepper to taste

Directions
1. Put the ground chicken in a bowl & mix in 1 tsp. of salt, 1 tbsp. of black pepper & 1 tbsp. of garlic powder.
2. Put a skillet on medium & spray some Pam.
3. Sautee mushrooms, garlic & onion in the pan.
4. When the onions are clear add the tomatoes, parsley, oregano & basil.
5. Set the heat on low & add 1/four C of water. Let the sauce simmer, whereas stirring often.
6. In one other pan, brown the chicken on medium heat. Drain any fat.
7. When the meat is finished, add it to the sauce & stir everything together.
8. Serve on top of spaghetti squash.

Lemon Curry Halibut

Ingredients

500g of
5 fresh halibut filets (100g each)
¾ of lemon juice
1 tbsp. of chili powder
1 tbsp. oregano
1 tbsp. garlic powder
1 tbsp. yellow curry powder

salt & pepper (to taste)

Directions
1. Mix all of the spices together.
2. Spray Pam on a medium heated pan.
3. Put the fillets on the pan & sprinkle them with half of the spice mix.
4. Cook for about 2 minutes.
5. Flip the fillets & sprinkle the rest of the spice mix on top.
6. Cook till the fillets are easily flaked.

Tuna Burgers

Ingredients

2 cans of tuna (in water)
½ C oats
2 egg whites
¼ C of finely chopped onions
onion & garlic powder to taste
1 tsp. chili flakes
½ C fat free plain Greek yogurt

Directions
1. Mix tuna, oats & egg whites in a bowl.
2. Mix in the spices, Greek yogurt & onions.
3. Form the combination into four patties.
4. Put the burgers on a skillet sprayed with Pam.
5. Cook for two minutes on all sides.

Goes nice on a toasted Ezekiel bread brushed with mustard. In case you are in a low carb zone merely smear lettuce leaves with mustard & enjoy!

Spicy Chicken Breast Chili

Ingredients

400g chicken breast, cubed.
2 cans of tomatoes
16oz tomato paste
1 C chopped green chilies
1 medium chopped onion
tbsp. chili seasoning
salt (to taste)

Directions
1. Spray Pam on a pan & brown the meat.
2. Whereas the meat is browning mix the remaining of the ingredients in a sauce pan & begin simmering.
3. Once the meat has browned (it should not be cooked) add it to the remaining of the ingredients in the saucepan.
4. Simmer for forty five minutes.

Round four weeks out we cut out the tomatoes & onions from our food plan, as they comprise a little extra carbs. Nonetheless, before that mark we enjoy this scrumptious dish every weekend!

Baked Sweet French Fries

Ingredients

2-three large sweet potatoes

1 tsp. Coconut Oil
1 tsp. ground garlic
1 tsp. ground chili
salt (to taste)

Directions
1. Cut the potatoes right into a French fry form.
2. Lightly spray them with Pam & mix.
3. Add the spices & mix once more.
4. Place the fries on a baking dish in a single layer.
5. Bake for 1 hour on 375.

YouCserve this recipe with our Dill Garlic Dip (pg. 116).

Frittata

Ingredients

100g sweet potato peeled & finely sliced
½ C of mushrooms finely sliced
¼ C of red onion finely chopped
1 whole egg
2 egg whites
1oz Fat Free Cheese

Directions
1. Place the sweet potato, onion & mushrooms on a non-stick pan & sauté till soft. Put apart on a plate or in a bowl.
2. Beat together the egg & egg whites & pour right into a hot non-stick pan.
3. Wait till the bottom units & add to the frittata the veggies which have been sautéed on top of it.

4. Add the grated cheese & transfer the pan to a hot grill to set the top & to melt the cheese.

Fettuccini Alfredo

Ingredients

four large zucchinis (Peeled & cut like spaghetti – utilizing a vegetable peeler) or you should use spaghetti squash
1 C of broccoli florets
2 tsp. olive oil
200g chicken breast (cut in cubes)
2 clove of garlic mined
2 tbsp. oat flour

½ C unsweetened almond milk
½ C water
2 cloves garlic
1 tsp. Italian seasoning
1 tsp. Invoice's Finest Chik'nish Seasoning (or other broth mix)
¼ tsp. salt (optional)
Black pepper -- to taste
2 tbsp. cornstarch -- MIXED WITH 2 tbsp. water

Directions
Make the pasta:
1. Utilizing a vegetable peeler, peel zucchini into long strips & place in a big bowl. Put aside
   Make the sauce:

2. Mix almond milk, garlic, water, seasonings, & broth mix in small saucepan over medium heat. Bring to boil after which add the cornstarch/water combination, stirring consistently till thickened. Put aside

   Make the chicken:
3. In the meantime, heat oil in a big pan over medium heat & add the chicken, broccoli & garlic & cook for three-5 minutes.
4. Once the chicken is golden brown on all sides, add the flour, salt & black pepper & stir to coat. Cook absolutely.
5. Add Alfredo sauce, stirring it always. Simmer for 1-2 minutes till the sauce bubbles.

   Bring it together:
6. Pour the sauce & chicken combination over the zucchini strips. Toss together till evenly mixed.

Garlic Lime Chicken Fajitas

Ingredients

1 tsp. Dehydrated mined garlic
1 tsp. dehydrated mined onion
1 tsp. ground cumin
1 tsp. dried oregano
2 tbsp. fresh cilantro (or 1 tsp. dry cilantro)
½ tsp. coarse black pepper
three tbsp. lime juice
1 tbsp orange juice
2 packets stevia
2 tbsp. coconut oil
½ tsp. sea salt
1.5 lbs. boneless skinless chicken breast cut into thin strips

1 red pepper
1 green pepper
1 yellow onion

Directions
1. Mix all of the ingredients besides the peppers & onion in a big bowl & mix till the chicken is totally coated.
2. Refrigerate no less than half-hour in order that the chicken is well marinated.
3. Once the chicken has been marinated, heat a big non-stick skillet on medium high heat & stir fry the chicken for a couple of minutes till lightly brown. Remove from pan & put aside.
4. Add peppers & onion & cook for about 5 minutes or till tender.
5. Add the chicken to the pepper & onion mix for a few more minutes till totally cooked.

Fish Muffins

Ingredients

1C of 6 oz. tuna
1/three C of oats
three egg whites
1 tbsp. fresh coriander chopped
1 green onion chopped
Salt & pepper to taste

Directions
1. In a medium sized pan sauté green onions till soft & take away from heat.

2. In a big bowl mix all ingredients together & make into one or two patties.
3. Coat a pan with oil or spray with non-stick cooking spray & sauté patties till browned on both sides.

Stuffed Tomatoes with Cottage Cheese & Egg

Ingredients

2 large tomatoes
three egg whites
½ C cottage cheese
1 C spinach
1 stalk green onions, chopped
2 cloves minced garlic
1 stalk parsley, chopped
1 tbsp. dried oregano
Salt & pepper (to taste)

Directions
1. Preheat oven to 425 degrees Celsius.
2. Cut the tomatoes' tops & scoop out the flesh.
3. Place the tomatoes bottom up on a baking dish & bake for five minutes
4. Sautee green onions, garlic, parsley & spinach
5. In the meantime, take the tomatoes out & sprinkle with salt
6. In a bowl, mix cottage cheese, add sautéed greens, oregano, salt & pepper.
7. Stuff the tomatoes with the combination, leaving some room for the egg whites.
8. Place the tomatoes back on the baking dish & put in the oven for added eight minutes.

9. Take out & serve.
10. (Optional) youCadd additional spices on top of the egg white & enjoy.

Baked Broccoli Loaf

Ingredients

eight c broccoli florets, steamed
four egg whites
2 c unsweetened almond milk
6 tbsp. ground flax seeds
½ tsp. baking powder
1 ½ c fat free cottage cheese

Directions
1. Preheat oven to 375 degrees Celsius.
2. In a bowl beat egg whites & cottage cheese.
3. Add almond milk, ground flax seeds, baking powder & broccoli & mix.
4. Bake for half-hour, or till the crust begins to form.
5. Remove from oven, cool it, & enjoy it!

Mushroom Burgers with Shrimp

Ingredients

200g cooked shrimp
four large Portobello mushroom caps
1 leek, finely chopped
2 tbsp. ground flax seeds
2 egg whites

1 tbsp. Worcestershire sauce
1 clove garlic, crushed
½ tsp. onion powder
four tbsp. fat free low sodium cottage cheese
Salt & pepper (to taste)

Directions
1. Preheat oven to 450.
2. Put the mushroom caps on a baking sheet sprayed with Pam.
3. Spray the mushroom caps with Pam & add salt & pepper.
4. Bake the mushroom caps for 12 minutes.
5. In a bowl mix egg white, leek, Worcestershire sauce, ground flax seeds, garlic, onion powder, salt & pepper.
6. Finely chop the cooked shrimp & add them into the bowl.
7. Mix the ingredients.
8. Divide the combination into two equal patties.
9. In a skillet sprayed with Pam, cook the patties for five minutes on all sides.
10. Put 2 tbsps. of cottage cheese into two mushroom caps, put the patties on top of the cottage cheese & top it off with the leftover mushroom caps.
11. Place in the over for an additional 5 minutes to melt the cottage cheese.
12. Remove from oven, cool it, enjoy!

Spicy Mexican Stir Fry

Ingredients

three skinless, boneless 150g chicken breasts, cut into cubes
three tbsp. chili powder
three medium red bell peppers, diced
1 large onion
2 Serrano peppers, minced
1 Jalapeno pepper, minced
1 large tomato, diced
Salt & pepper (to taste)

Directions
1. Heat up a big skillet sprayed with Pam.
2. Add chicken, 1 tbsp. of chili powder, salt & pepper.
3. Brown the meat till no longer pink.
4. Remove the chicken from the skillet.
5. In the same skillet, sauté the peppers & the onion.
6. Add Serrano's, Jalapeno, tomato & a couple of tbsps. of chili powder
7. Stir-fry the greens for three minutes.
8. Add the chicken & stir-fry for two more minutes.
9. Remove from heat & enjoy

It's a easy low fat recipe that may be served over brown rice or sweet potatoes, or just eaten by itself. It's scrumptious anyway you serve it!

African Style Vegetable Medley

Ingredients

1 large onion, cut in strips
5 cloves of garlic, minced
2 tsp. ground cumin
1 tbsp. fresh ginger, grated
1 tsp. hot paprika

½ tsp. turmeric
three tbsp. freshly squeezed lemon juice
2 bay leaves
2lb cauliflower florets, cut into 2" pieces
30oz canned diced tomatoes
15oz canned chickpeas, drained
1 tbsp. cinnamon
1 large zucchini, cut into 1" pieces
1/three c fresh cilantro

Directions
1. Heat up a big pan & spray it with Pam.
2. Sautee onion & cook till it's translucent.
3. Add garlic, paprika, cumin, ginger, bay leaves, lemon juice, salt & pepper, cooking the greens till soft.
4. Add 2 cups of water, cauliflower, diced tomatoes (with the juices), chickpeas & cinnamon.
5. Bring everything to a boil.
6. Reduce the heat to low, cover & simmer for quarter-hour, stirring every three-four minutes.
7. Add zucchini & cook for 10 more minutes, till zucchini is soft.
8. Remove from heat & let cool for 10-quarter-hour.

This recipe goes nice on top of brown rice or quinoa & chicken breast on the side. YouCeven add some chili flakes, in case you prefer it spicy.

Pasta Free Lasagna

Ingredients

1lb of extra lean ground turkey
1lb zucchini, thinly sliced
1 c fat free low sodium cottage cheese

1C of crushed tomatoes
1 large onion, chopped
three cloves of garlic, minced
2 c chopped spinach
1 tsp. dried sage
1 tsp. dried oregano
1 tsp. dried rosemary
1 tsp. dried thyme
1 c fat free sour cream
2 egg whites
2 c broccoli florets, steamed & chopped

Directions
1. Preheat oven to 375.
2. In a pan sprayed with Pam, brown the meat, drain it & put apart.
3. In the same pan sauté onion & garlic.
4. Once the onion is translucent, add in the meat, crushed tomatoes, seasonings & spinach.
5. In a bowl, mix sour cream, egg whites & broccoli. Add salt & pepper (optional).
6. In a big baking dish, layer the bottom with a half of the zucchini slices
7. Top the zucchini with half of the sour cream sauce & add half of the meat sauce on top of it.
8. Repeat the same process once more; 1 more layer of zucchini, 1 more layer of sour cream, 1 more layer of meat sauce.
9. Spread the cottage cheese on top of the lasagna.
10. Cover the goodness with a tin foil & bake for 50 minutes.
11. Take the tin foil off & bake for added 10 minutes.
12. Remove from the oven, let cool & serve!

Chicken Shawarma Lettuce Wraps

What you need

1 C shredded English cucumber
¼ C non-fat plain Greek yogurt
1 tbsp. tahini
2 tbsp.s lemon juice
½ tsp. salt, divided
1 tbsp. garlic powder
1 tsp. curry powder
½ tsp. freshly ground pepper
1 pound boneless, skinless chicken breast, trimmed
1 tbsp. coconut oil
Large romaine lettuce leaves

Directions
1. Preheat grill to medium.
2. Stir cucumber, yogurt, tahini, lemon juice & 1/four tsp. salt together in a medium bowl. Put aside.
3. Mix garlic powder, curry powder, pepper & the remaining 1/four tsp. salt in one other medium bowl. Slice chicken breast crosswise into 1/four-inch strips; toss with the spice combination to coat. Add 1 tbsp. oil & toss to mix.
4. Grill the chicken, turning once, till cooked through, about 2 minutes per side.
5. To serve, spread 1/four C of the cucumber-yogurt sauce on a big lettuce leaf & top with one-fourth of the chicken. Fold like a taco & enjoy!

Tuna Cucumber Roll

Ingredients

¼ English cucumber
1C tuna
½ avocado
2 tbsp. of mustard (yellow or Dijon)
salt & pepper (to taste)

Directions
1. In a bowl, mix tuna, mustard & avocado.
2. Cut the cucumber into ½ inch thick slices.
3. Discard the centres of the cucumber slices (either cut them out with a knife, or push them out with your fingers).
4. Stuff the hollow centered cucumbers with the tuna mix.
5. Add salt & pepper & enjoy!

Asian Salmon Steaks

Ingredients:

6 (5 ounce) fillets salmon or tilapia
four tbsp.s low-sodium fermented soy sauce
four tbsp.s balsamic vinegar
four tbsp.s green onions, chopped
three packets stevia
four cloves garlic, minced
1 ½ tsp.s ground ginger
2 tsp.s crushed red pepper flakes
1 tsp. sesame oil

½ tsp. salt

Directions
1. Place salmon fillets in a medium, nonporous glass dish. In a separate medium bowl, mix soy sauce, vinegar, green onions, stevia, garlic, ginger, red pepper flakes, sesame oil & salt. Whisk together, & pour over the fish. Cover & marinate the fish in the fridge for four to six hours.
2. Prepare an out of doors grill with coals about 5 inches from the grate, & lightly oil the grate.
3. Grill the fillets 5 inches from coals for 10 minutes per inch of thickness, measured at the thickest part, or till fish just flakes with a fork. Turn over midway through cooking.

Sushi

Ingredients

2-three Roasted Seaweed Nori Sheets
1C of low-sodium white tuna (in water)
2 tbsp. low-sodium fermented soy sauce
½ tsp. sesame oil (optional)
2 tbsp. chopped green onions
1 tsp. chili powder
2 + 2 tbsp. Fat Free Mayo (see recipe on web page 116) - or Dijon Mustard
2 Tbsp. Rice vinegar
¼ cucumber (cut lengthwise into match sticks)
Wasabi paste (optional)

Directions

1. Mix tuna, soy sauce, sesame oil, green onion, chili powder, 2 tbsp. mayo, & rice vinegar together in a bowl.
2. Lay nori sheets flat one after the other on a cutting board. Spread 1 tbsp. mayo to cover the whole sheet in a thin layer. ThisCsoften the nori sheet so that they don't break &Chelp you get them to stay once you roll them.
3. Add tuna combination in the middle lengthwise.
4. Add cucumber matchsticks.
5. Add wasabi if desired.
6. Roll nori sheets right into a tube/wrap style. Greatest to eat like a wrap or hand roll (in case you select to chop into maki style, use a very sharp knife & ensure the wrap is very tight.
7. YouCeven get some pickled ginger & have it on the side.

Chicken Tacos Salad

Ingredients

300g of extra lean ground chicken or turkey
½ large yellow onion chopped
½ red pepper chopped
1 tsp. oregano
2 tsp. chili pepper
½ tsp. black pepper
1 packet stevia
1 smallCof diced tomatoes drained (herb & garlic flour is good – no oil!)
Salt to taste
6 leaves of romaine lettuce

Directions
1. Spray a medium sized pot with PAM & heat on mid high heat.
2. Add onions & peppers & cook till onions are clear.
3. Add all other ingredients apart from canned tomatoes & lettuce
4. Mix everything together in the pot & cook till the ground chicken/turkey is completed.
5. Remove from heat & drain any extra liquid.
6. Bring it back on the stovetop, reduce heat to medium low & add the canned tomatoes.
7. Cook an additional 5 minutes. Remove from stove & serve.
8. You should use romaine leaves as "taco" shells & add chicken combination inside each leaf or just chop up the lettuce & add combination on top & function a salad.

Tom Soup

Ingredients

6 cups organic chicken/beef or vegetable broth/stock
2 tbsp. frozen prepared lemongrass
three-four lime leaves
three-four cloves garlic minced
1 thumb-size piece of ginger
three tbsp. fish sauce or four tbsp. soy sauce (use wheat-free soy sauce for gluten-free diets)
1 tbsp. fresh lime juice
1 fresh red chili, or ½ tsp. dried crushed chili

greens of your choice (mushrooms, cauliflower, bok choy, broccoli)
30 shrimp or three chicken breasts (cooked)
½C coconut milk
½ C fresh basil and/or ½ C fresh coriander (cilantro)

Directions
1. Mix first four ingredients together & let boil.
2. Bring the heat to low-medium & add everything besides the last three ingredients.
3. Simmer for quarter-hour or so (till the greens are cooked to your liking).
4. Add coconut milk & your meat.
5. Let cook one other three-5 minutes (till it lightly bubbles once more).
6. For final touch fill up with cilantro or basil when serving in bowls.

Bun-Much less Mushroom Cheese Burgers

Ingredients

500g of extra lean ground turkey
three oz. Allegro four% cheese, chopped
½ C sun-dried tomatoes, drained & chopped
2 cloves garlic, minced
2 tsp. cumin powder
eight large Portobello mushrooms (stem removed) *for "burger buns"*
cooking spray

Directions

1. Mix first 5 ingredients together in a big bowl. Lightly mix together & form into four patties.
2. Heat a big pan over medium high add oil or cooking spray & cook the patties about 5-6 minutes on both sides (lightly cut in the center to be certain that they're totally cooked). Remove from heat.
3. Clean the pan & add oil or cooking spray once more & grill the Portobello mushrooms several minutes on all sides till tender. Remove from heat.
4. Place each of the burger patties on a grilled mushroom cap, add shredded cabbage & use other burger toppings you would like.
5. Place second mushroom cap on top.

Chicken Meatloaf

Ingredients

2.5lb of extra lean ground chicken
1 medium onion
1 green pepper
½ c zucchini
½ c broccoli
2 stems of celery
1 c mushrooms
1 tbsp. thyme
¼ c fresh basil
¼ c fresh parsley
salt & pepper (to taste)
four egg whites
2 c organic rolled oats
1 clove minced garlic

Directions

1. In a skillet sprayed with Pam, sauté onions, pepper, zucchini, broccoli, celery & mushrooms till tender.
2. Add garlic 1-2 minutes before the greens are done, remove from heat & cool them off for about 5 minutes.
3. In a big bowl, mix the remaining of the ingredients with the sautéed greens.
4. Put the combination into loaf pans or any baking dish sprayed with Pam.
5. Put in an oven on 425 degrees Celsius for forty minutes.
6. Remove from the oven & let the meatloaf sit for forty five minutes.
7. Slice into eight pieces & enjoy.

Breadless Crab Truffles

Ingredients

8oz crab meat, canned
2 egg whites
2 tsp. Worcestershire sauce
1 tbsp. freshly squeezed lemon juice
1 tsp. Tarragon
three tbsp. of our Dill Garlic Dip (see recipe on web page 117)
Salt & pepper (to taste)

Directions
1. Turn oven to broil.
2. In a bowl, mix egg whites, seasonings & the Dill Garlic Dip.

3. Divide the combination in two & form them into two balls.
4. Put the crab balls right into a baking dish sprayed with pam & broil for eight minutes
5. Remove from oven, cool it, & enjoy it!

Grilled Citrus Flavored Chicken Breast

Ingredients

5 medium skinless, boneless chicken breast halves (roughly 100g each)
¼ c balsamic vinegar
2 cloves of fresh garlic, crushed
¼ tsp. black pepper
½ medium size lemon, peeled & cubed
three tbsp. Dijon mustard

Directions
1. Mix all of the ingredients, besides chicken breast.
2. Pour the ingredients over chicken, cover & refrigerate overnight.
3. Drain the marinade.
4. Grill the chicken for five minutes on all sides on high heat.
5. Serve with your carbs or greens & enjoy!

Shrimp Stuffed Tomato

Ingredients

300g of cooked shrimp
three tbsp. of fat free plain Greek yogurt
1 tsp. dried dill
three medium tomatoes
Salt & pepper (to taste)
1 c spinach, finely chopped

Directions
1. In a blender, mix the shrimp, yogurt, spices & spinach.
2. Core the tomatoes.
3. Stuff the tomatoes with the shrimp combination & sprinkle some salt on top, if needed.

Grilled Balsamic Basa

Ingredients

four 100g basa fillets
1 tbsp. fresh rosemary, chopped
Salt & pepper (to taste)
½ c balsamic vinegar
1 tbsp. extra virgin olive oil
four tbsp. lemon juice, freshly squeezed
four c baby spinach

Directions
1. In a bowl, mix the vinegar, lemon juice & olive oil.
2. Pour the marinade over the salmon & refrigerate for 1.5 hours.
3. Remove from the fridge & sprinkle spices & rosemary over the fish.

4. Grill for about 5 minutes on both sides, till the fillets begin to flake.
5. Serve over baby spinach.

Mustard & Dill Broiled Salmon

Ingredients

5 tbsp. zero fat plain Greek yogurt
2 tbsp. Dijon mustard
2 tbsp. fresh dill, chopped
four cloves fresh garlic, minced
four tbsp. freshly squeezed lemon juice
½ tsp. chili powder
four 150g salmon fillets

Directions

1. Preheat broiler.
2. In a small bowl, mix Greek yogurt, mustard, dill, garlic, lemon juice & chili powder.
3. Place the salmon on the broiler pan sprayed with Pam.
4. Pour the sauce over the salmon & place it three inches beneath the broiler's heat supply.
5. Broil for five-6 minutes.
6. Reduce the heat to 425 degrees Celsius, turn off the broiler & bake the salmon for six-7 minutes more.
7. Remove from the oven & serve.

Grilled Tomato Shrimp

Ingredients

2 cloves garlic, minced
four tbsp. olive oil
1 medium tomato, cubed
1 tbsp. red wine vinegar
2 tbsp. fresh basil, chopped
Salt & pepper (to taste)
1lb of fresh peeled shrimp

Directions
1. Mix garlic, olive oil, tomato, vinegar, basil, salt & pepper in a blender.
2. Pour the combination right into a bowl & add the shrimp.
3. Put the bowl in the fridge for an hour.
4. Preheat the grill on medium heat.
5. Place the shrimp on skewers.
6. Spray Pam on the grill & grill the shrimp for two minutes on either side.

Enjoy this scrumptious dish with the side dish of your choice.

Grilled Chicken Breast with Veggie Salsa

Ingredients

2 4oz Chicken Breasts
2 cups Cherry tomatoes
2 cups Zucchini
1 C Broccoli
2 tbsp. Coriander
2 c. Celery

1 clove Garlic, minced
1 C Onion
2 cups Mushrooms
1 tsp. Ginger
1 tsp. Chili
Lime Juice, to taste

Directions
1. Grill Chicken breast till cooked through
2. Utilizing a non stick pan add garlic, onion, chili, lime juice, ginger, mushrooms, zucchini, & cherry tomatoes.
3. Once they've cooked add the broccoli & celery & cook for added three-5 minutes, leaving the greens a little bit crunchy.
4. Add the coriander & more lime juice as required.

Tip: Use a bigger amount of greens, if you wish to save a few of the scrumptious salsa for later!

Turkey Breast Quick Wraps

Ingredients

50g thinly sliced smoked turkey breast.
30g Allegro cheese, shredded
Iceberg Lettuce Leaves
Broccoli sprouts
½ thinly sliced avocado
Cayenne pepper

Directions
1. Put all of the ingredients into the lettuce wraps & add Cayenne pepper at the very finish.
2. Enjoy!

Mexican Rissoles

Ingredients
For Salsa:

Finely chopped:
1 medium tomato
¼ of enormous cucumber
¼ red onion
half avocado
juice from ½ a lime
chili powder to taste
Iceberg lettuce

For Rissoles:

500g of ground beef
1 chopped medium onion
2 cloves of garlic minced
¼ C of almond meal
chili to taste

Directions
1. Dice all salsa ingredients, mix in a bowl & refrigerate.
2. Sautee onion & let it cool.
3. Mix in a bowl beef, almond meal & chili.
4. Once your onion has cooled down add it to the combination & mix everything together.
5. Roll the combination into 10 balls & cook on a low heat in the pan sprayed with Pam.
6. Put a layer of Salsa on a lettuce leaf.
7. Add three rissoles & enjoy!

Cucumber Radish Dill Salad

Ingredients

1 medium cucumber
¼ tsp. salt
2 large spring onions (scallions) with green stems, finely sliced
four medium red radishes, thinly sliced
½ C fat free Greek yogurt
2 tbsp. white wine vinegar
1 tbsp. finely chopped fresh dill or 1 tsp. dried dill
1 packet stevia
1 tsp. Dijon mustard
¼ tsp. freshly ground black pepper

Directions

1. Slice cucumber in half & scoop out the seeds with a spoon.
2. Place in a bowl & sprinkle with salt & let stand half-hour (salting cucumbers removes a few of the liquid in order that the flavour of a dressing shouldn't be closely diluted).
3. Drain & pat dry.
4. Chop cucumber, spring onions & radishes & mix in a big bowl.
5. Make dressing by combing & whisking together, vinegar, dill, stevia, mustard & pepper till mixed.
6. Spoon dressing over cucumber combination & toss to coat.
7. Cover & refrigerate one hour.

Fresh Quinoa Salad

Ingredients

1 C quinoa
2 C of water
1 clove of garlic, minced
1 medium bay leaf
Salt & pepper (to taste)
1 tbsp. extra virgin olive oil
2 tbsp. freshly squeezed lemon juice
1 C cucumber, diced
½ C green onion

Directions
1. Rinse quinoa in cold water for four-5 minutes
2. Put water, garlic, bay leaf, salt & pepper in a sauce pan & bring to a boil.
3. Stir in quinoa & reduce heat to medium. Cook for about quarter-hour. Remove quinoa from heat & cool it for quarter-hour.
4. Add olive oil, lemon juice, cucumber & onion & stir well.

Fresh Chicken Salad

Ingredients

450g of refrigerated grilled turkey, cubed
three c baby spinach
2 c lettuce
2 c fresh arugula
1 medium tomato, chopped
1 c green onion, chopped
four tbsp. balsamic vinegar

Directions
1. Toss all of the ingredients into a big bowl & mix all of them together.
2. Add salt & pepper to taste (optional).

Apple Cinnamon Protein Muffins

Ingredients

2 cups Oats
½ C of Oat Bran
12 Egg whites
1 scoop of Vanilla Protein Powder
½ tsp. of Baking Soda
5 packets stevia
2 diced Apples - per bowl, grams
four Tbsp. of Unsweetened Apple Sauce
1 tsp. of Cinnamon
1 tsp. of Vanilla Extract

Directions
1. Preheat the oven for 350 degrees.
2. In a blender, mix all of the ingredients (aside from the diced apple), till combination is thick.
3. Add the diced apple & stir (with a spoon or a spatula).
4. Poor the combination in a muffin cooking pan, & bake at 350 for about half-hour.

Protein Bars

Ingredients

6 tbsp. unsweetened shredded coconut

6 tbsp.¼ C almond flour (purchase at a well being food store or make your personal by mixing almonds)

three tbsp.½ C ground flax seeds
1/three tbsp.cup chopped walnuts
¼ C natural sweetener like Stevia
eight scoops chocolate whey protein powder
four large table spoons of natural almond butter
½ C unsweetened almond milk

Directions
1. Mix all dry ingredients together. Add almond butter & mix till everything sticks together. Lastly, add a little bit of almond milk slowly till you get sticky mix (not too gooey) barely enough so that youCform it into a giant flat pancake form that wont crumble.
2. Spray some non stick oil spray right into a sq. or rectangular pan, & sprinkle shredded coconut at the bottom.
3. Spread the combination onto the pan, you'll have to make use of your hands.
4. Lastly, sprinkle with some more shredded coconut on top as well in order that it's not too sticky later.
5. Refrigerate for a few hours, & when the combination is good & firm, cut into squares.

Dairy Free Protein Bars

Ingredients

6 tbsp. cups unsweetened shredded coconut

6 tbsp. ¼ C almond flour (purchase at a well being food store or make your personal by mixing almonds)

three tbsp. ½ C ground flax seeds

¼ C natural sweetener like Stevia – you should utilize flavoured liquid vanilla too

four tbsp. unsweetened cocoa powder

eight scoops chocolate whey protein powder

½ C a hundred% Pure Pumpkin (canned)

½ C Unsweetened almond milk

Directions

1. Mix all dry ingredients together. Add almond butter & mix until everything sticks together. Lastly add a little bit of almond milk slowly till you get sticky mix (not too gooey) barely enough so that youCform into a giant flat pancake form that will not crumble.
2. Spray some non-stick oil spray right into a sq. or rectangular pan, & sprinkle shredded coconut at the bottom.
3. Spread the combo into the pan.
4. Lastly sprinkle with some more shredded coconut on top as well in order that it's not too sticky later.
5. Refrigerate for a few hours, & when the combination is sweet & firm, cut into squares.

Protein Cupcakes

Ingredients

eight egg whites

1 scoop of protein powder (banana flavor is the most effective)
1tbsp of cocoa powder
1tsp cinnamon
¼ C oat bran
three-four packets of stevia

Directions
1. Preheat the oven to 350
2. Mix the egg whites, protein powder, cinnamon, stevia & the cocoa powder together in a blender.
3. Pour the combination in a cupcake dish, filling ¾ of every socket.
4. Bake for half-hour. The cupcakes needs to be very fluffy & puff out of their sockets.
5. Take out of the oven & cool for 10 minutes
6. Enjoy!

Gluten, Carb & Dairy Free Bread

Ingredients

300g almond meal
four tbsp. olive oil
1 tsp. baking powder
6 egg whites
stevia to taste
2 tsp. of cinnamon

Directions
1. Mix all of the ingredients together to make a dough.
2. Form right into a loaf form into your baking tin.
3. Bake for round 30min on 200 degrees Celsius.

4. Let the loaf cool for 20 minutes & take away from tin.
5. Enjoy!

Selfmade Protein Bars

Ingredients

2 ½ c. (200 g) oats
2 scoop (30 g) whey protein isolate (use chocolate flavor)
6 egg whites
2 medium bananas (300 g), mashed
1 tbsp. Honey
½ C almond milk
1 tsp. Cinnamon

Directions
1. Preheat the oven to 355.
2. Mix together the oats, whey & cinnamon.
3. Add egg whites, mashed bananas & honey.
4. Add lactose free skim milk slowly whereas mixing.
5. Spoon the combination right into a lined cake tin sprayed with Pam & degree with a knife.
6. Place in oven & bake for quarter-hour.
7. Remove from oven & permit to chill for five minutes.
8. Cut into four bars.

Protein Cinnamon Cake with Cocoa Syrup

Ingredients

5 scoops of protein powder
eight egg whites
1-2 tbsp. of cinnamon
¼ tsp. of baking powder
1 tsp. vanilla extract
Stevia to taste
100ml of water
1 tbsp. cocoa powder

Directions
Cake:
1. Mix the dry ingredients in a blender.
2. Add the egg whites to the combo.
3. Slowly add water. You are trying to find a smooth consistency, the combination shouldn't be runny.
4. Pour the combination right into a microwave pleasant dish & cover.
5. Microwave for four minutes.
6. Cool the cake for 10-quarter-hour.

Syrup:
1. Mix stevia, cocoa powder & 1 tsp. of cinnamon
2. Add a few drops of water. Little or no, so the consistency just isn't runny.
3. Pour it on top of the cake
4. Serve & Enjoy!

Frozen Yogurt

Ingredients

¾ C of Greek yogurt
1 tbsp. crushed flax seeds
1 scoop whey protein isolate (any flavor)
Stevia (optional)
Carb & fat free pudding powder

Directions
1. Mix all of the ingredients together.
2. Put in the freezer for two-three hours.
3. Take out & enjoy!

Blueberry Cookies

Ingredients

eight egg whites
1 C blueberries
1 C oat flour (merely mix the oats in a blender)
2 scoops of whey isolate protein powder (vanilla works greatest)
¼ tsp. baking powder

Directions
1. Mix all of the ingredients, besides blueberries, in a bowl & mix well.
2. Add the blueberries & mix them with the remaining of the ingredients.

3. Spoon the dough & put it on a baking dish (ought to make 20 cookies).
4. Bake on 375 F for 12 minutes or till crispy.

Cinnamon Oatmeal High Protein Frozen Pudding

Ingredients

½ C oatmeal
1 scoop of favourite Whey Protein Powder (Vanilla or Chocolate flavor)
three packets of Stevia
Cinnamon

Directions
1. Mix all of the ingredients right into a bowl.
2. Add water.
3. Place in the freezer to chill for 30 to 60 min.
4. Enjoy your high protein frozen pudding.

Veggie & Egg Muffins

Ingredients

1 lbs. mushrooms (thinly sliced)
three cups steamed broccoli (cut into small pieces)
a hundred & fifty g Allégro Cheese (four% - any flavor – grated)
four green onions (chopped)

1 tsp. Italian Seasoning
1 tsp. garlic powder
Salt & pepper to taste
1.5 tsp. olive oil
6 whole eggs
6 egg whites
Muffin tray

Directions
1. Preheat over at 350°F.
2. Meanwhile spray a big pan with non-stick spray, & sauté mushrooms & onions on high heat till browned.
3. Whereas the mushrooms are cooking, place steamed broccoli in large bowl, add olive oil, Italian seasoning & garlic powder & mash with a fork till chunky.
4. Once the mushrooms are done, add them to the broccoli, mix & put aside to chill.
5. Once room temperature add the grated cheese salt & pepper.
6. Spray muffin tray with non-stick cooking spray & add the broccoli, mushroom, cheese combination ¾ full (ought to have enough for six muffins).
7. Now beat eggs & egg whites in a bowl till fluffy, add salt & pepper.
8. Pour egg combination over the greens in the muffin tin.
9. Bake 10-quarter-hour (till eggs set on top).
10. Enjoy! (these may be refrigerated or frozen for later use)

Zucchini Chips with Cajun Dip

Ingredients

For the Chips
2 large zucchini
1 tbsp. olive oil
¼ tsp. salt
½ garlic powder
½ tsp. chili powder
For the dip
1 C low fat cottage cheese
1.5 tbsp. Cajun Seasoning
(see condiments part for recipe or use industrial seasoning)

Directions
1. Preheat oven at 400°F.
2. Meanwhile, slice zucchini roughly 1/eight of an inch thick.
3. Place in a big bowl & toss with olive oil, salt, garlic powder, & chili powder.
4. Spray a big baking sheet (you might have two) with nonstick cooking spray like PAM, & arrange zucchini slices in a single layer.
5. Bake for 25mins turning often.
6. Reduce temperature to 300°F & bake till crisp (one other 10-15mins).
7. Whereas the zucchini is baking make the dip by mixing Cajun Seasoning with cottage cheese & place in fridge till prepared to make use of.
8. Once the zucchini is baked, remove from oven & place on paper towels & let it cool.

Protein Fudge Balls

Directions

three scoops of chocolate whey protein powder
1 C almond meal
50g desiccated coconut plus 10g extra for coating
1 tsp. peanut butter
50g unsweetened cocoa
four packets Stevia
Cold water

Directions
1. Mix all ingredients besides water & extra coconut for coating.
2. Knead together right into a paste, step by step adding water till it's dough-like.
3. Mould into 21 small balls & cover in additional coconut.

Hungarian Stew

Ingredients

2 lbs. (1") cubed veal
2 onions, white or yellow chopped very finely (the finer the higher!)
2-three garlic cloves minced
2tbsp Coconut Oil
2-three Tbsp. (adjust to taste) Hungarian sweet paprika

1 tsp. bay leaves
1 Qt. water or broth/stock
1 head cauliflower
¼ tsp. black pepper
1 tsp. salt
2 tsp. caraway seeds

Directions
1. Add 1 tbsp. of oil or butter to large pot & brown meat on high heat (just the surface of the meat needs to be browned, thisChelp keep the flavour & keep it moist). Put aside
2. Add 1 tbsp. of oil to a frying pan & fry onions on medium heat till soft.
3. Add garlic till browned.
4. Bring the pot with meat back to the stove & add the fried onions & garlic to it & set on medium heat.
5. Add all spices to water or broth/stock.
6. Cook for about 1.5 to 2 hrs. (for beef or veal), & 20-25mins for chicken.
7. The longer you cook the beef or veal the more tender it will likely be.
8. The liquid will become thicker.

Moroccan Style Chicken

Ingredients

½ tsp. cinnamon powder
1 tbsp. chili powder
1 tsp. paprika
1 tbsp. cumin powder

2 cloves of minced garlic
three tbsp. of olive oil (optional)
½ C red wine vinegar
1-2 medium onions – cut into long thin strips
eight (125g each) chicken skinless boneless chicken breasts

Directions

1. Preheat oven 350°F.
2. Mix all of the spices along with oil & vinegar & mix or mix together to make marinade.
3. Chop onions lengthwise into rings & put aside.
4. Place chicken breasts in a deep baking pan (preferably one which comes with a lid)
5. Pour marinade over chicken (its even greater in case you let the chicken marinade in the fridge for a few hours, but works either way) & add the onions.
6. Be sure that the chicken is evenly covered with marinade & onions.
7. Bake for 1 hour or till chicken is completed (check & switch pieces after 25 minutes after which check every 10 min).

Beef & Broccoli Stir Fry

Ingredients

2 tsp. coconut oil
6 cups broccoli cut into florets
four thinly sliced carrot
2 onion, cut into thin wedges
10 oz. sirloin steak cut into strips
6 tbsp. low sodium chicken or beef broth
2 tbsp. reduced sodium soy sauce

1 tsp. corn starch
2 packet Stevia

Directions
1. Heat coconut oil in a big skillet & add the chopped greens.
2. Sauté till veggies are crisp, tender & onions are browned. Put aside.
3. Stir in the beef strips, cook till desired tenderness.
4. In a separate bowl, mix broth, soy sauce, cornstarch, & stevia stirring to dissolve the cornstarch completely.
5. Add to the beef & veggie combination & cook stirring always till sauce thickens.

Easy Chicken & Spinach Stir Fry

Ingredients

four x 6 oz. boneless raw chicken breasts, diced
four c. raw spinach
three c. raw onion, sliced
1 red pepper
four tsp. coconut oil
6 cloves garlic
½ tsp. dash ground black pepper
four sprigs raw coriander
salt to taste

Directions

1. Put spinach, red pepper, onion, garlic salt & pepper in a non-stick pan with 2 tsp. of oil & cook till tender. Remove from heat & put aside.
2. In one other pan cook diced chicken in 2 tsp. of oil till lightly browned.
3. Add veggie combination to chicken & heat through.
4. Simmer whole combination for three-5 minutes.
5. Add coriander & stir.

Stuffed Chicken Breast

Ingredients

four 4oz chicken breasts
2 c diced mushrooms
2 c fresh spinach
2 large diced tomatoes
three cloves of minced garlic
1 large onion
1 c Greek yogurt
Salt & pepper (to taste)

Directions

1. Spray Pam on a medium heat skillet.
2. Add mushrooms, tomatoes, garlic, onions, Greek yogurt & spices.
3. Sautee the greens till tender & the onions are translucent.
4. Cut the chicken breasts horizontally to form a pocket in each one among them.
5. Stuff each chicken breast with fresh spinach & the sautéed greens.

6. Put in the oven & bake for 30-forty minutes on four hundred.

    This recipe goes well on a mattress of brown rice. If a number of the sautéed greens are left over youCput them on top of the rice, or simply eat them as a garnish if you're cutting carbs.

Russian Stir-Fry

Ingredients

200g chicken breast, cubed
1 tbsp. of chili garlic sauce
2 large cabbage leaves
1 c mushrooms
1 c spinach
200g boiled sweet potato

Directions
1. Brown the chicken in a skillet sprayed with Pam on medium heat.
2. Once the chicken is midway cooked, add the remaining of the ingredients.
3. Cover & cook for five-7 minutes on high.
4. Plate & enjoy!

Low Carb Tacos

Ingredients

200g of ground turkey
½ packet of taco seasoning
2 c green bell pepper, cubed

three tbsp. salsa
2 large romaine lettuce leaves
2 C tomato, diced
2oz Allegro cheese, shredded
1 c fat free sour cream

Directions
1. Brown the turkey in a skillet sprayed with Pam.
2. Add taco seasoning.
3. Stir in peppers & salsa.
4. Cook till the greens are tender.
5. Scoop the meat & greens & stuff the lettuce leaves.
6. Put 1-2 tbsp. of sour cream.
7. Sprinkle with cheese & enjoy!

Chicken Breast Mushroom Sandwich

Ingredients

1 c of sliced mushrooms
1 stalk of green onions, sliced
100g chicken breast, sliced horizontally right into a cutlet
2 slices of four:9 Ezekiel bread
Salt & pepper (to taste)
Dijon mustard
Calorie free hot sauce

Directions
1. Toast the Ezekiel bread.
2. In a pan sprayed with Pam, sauté mushrooms & onions with pepper & salt.

3. Once the greens are prepared, take them out of the pan & put apart.
4. Spray the skillet with Pam & cook the chicken breast, adding salt & pepper.
5. Because the chicken breast is getting fried, sprinkle some hot sauce on one slice of toast & mustard on the opposite.
6. On the toast sprinkled with hot sauce, mount the greens.
7. Once the chicken is prepared, put it on top of the greens & top it off with the opposite piece of toast.

Cheese Wraps

Ingredients

1 c zero fat cottage cheese
½ avocado
1 clove garlic, minced
2 tbsp. freshly squeezed lemon juice
½ tsp. jalapeno pepper, minced
½ a stalk green onion, minced
Salt & pepper (to taste)

Directions
1. Scoop out avocado flesh.
2. Put all of the ingredients in a blender. Mix till you get a smooth puree.
3. Wrap in a lettuce leaf & serve.

Printed in Great Britain
by Amazon